ARCTIC ADVENTURE

by Caren B. Stelson

illustrated by Alex Farquharson

Scott Foresman

Editorial Offices: Glenview, Illinois • New York, New York
Sales Offices: Reading, Massachusetts • Duluth, Georgia
Glenview, Illinois • Carrollton, Texas • Menlo Park, California

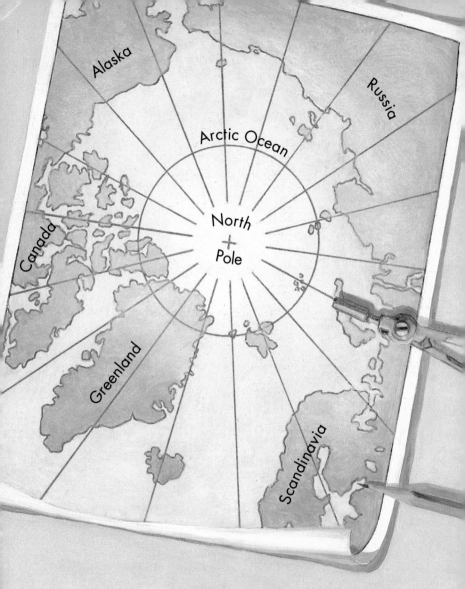

This is the Arctic—the crown of the world. The
Arctic is a land of ice. Come on this Arctic
adventure! Explore the region as others have before
you. You will discover this is a world like no other.

2

Please do not confuse the Arctic with Antarctica. The Arctic is at the top of the world. Antarctica lies at the bottom. Antarctica is a large continent of land. The Arctic region is quite different. This is a large ocean. It is two miles deep and surrounded by eight nations.

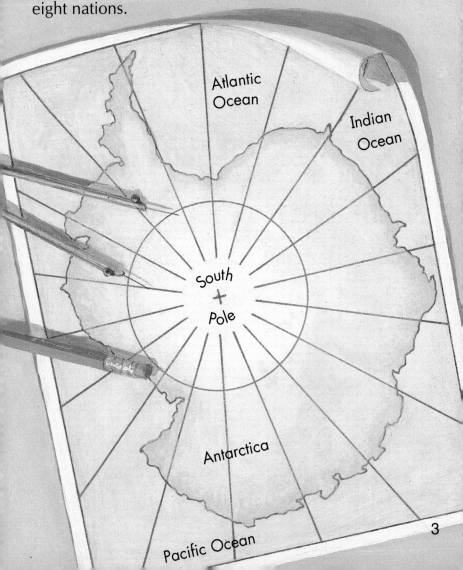

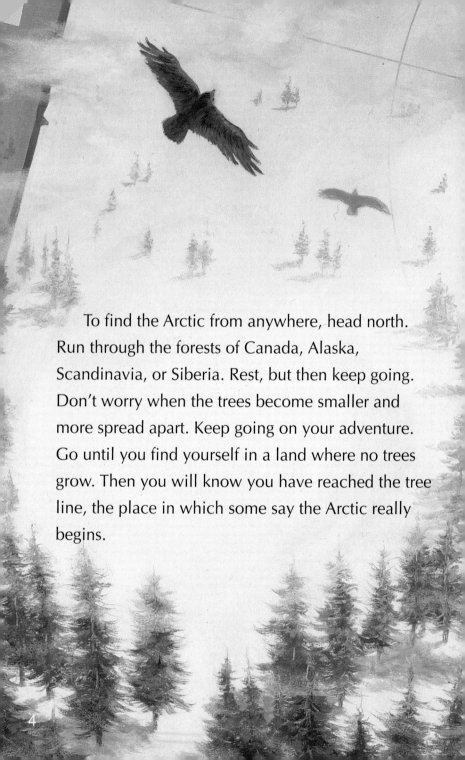

To find the Arctic from anywhere, head north. Run through the forests of Canada, Alaska, Scandinavia, or Siberia. Rest, but then keep going. Don't worry when the trees become smaller and more spread apart. Keep going on your adventure. Go until you find yourself in a land where no trees grow. Then you will know you have reached the tree line, the place in which some say the Arctic really begins.

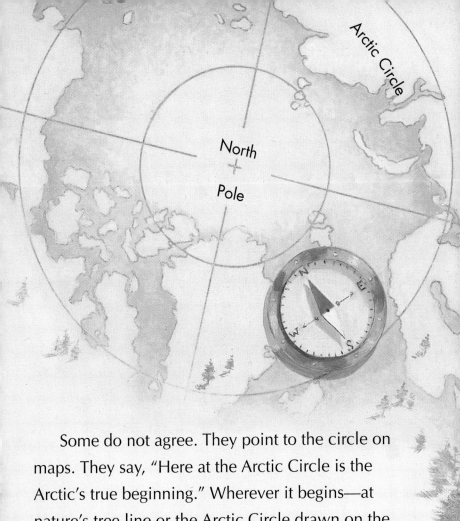

North
+
Pole

Arctic Circle

Some do not agree. They point to the circle on maps. They say, "Here at the Arctic Circle is the Arctic's true beginning." Wherever it begins—at nature's tree line or the Arctic Circle drawn on the map—it is the same. The air is cold. The ground is frozen. There is not enough light for even one tree to grow.

Those who know the Arctic say it is the worst in winter. It can wrap you in darkness for five months of the year, with only a bit of light. Stay until December 21st or 22nd, if you can. The winter solstice comes then. That's the shortest day of the year. On that day, above the Arctic Circle, there is no sunrise at all. It is entirely dark.

You might say, "I can live with darkness." Maybe so, but can you live with the cold winds? The Arctic's wind can freeze you with winter temperatures that can sink to sixty degrees below zero. It can whip you with winds that blow over fifty miles an hour.

The Arctic is gentler in spring. Its temperatures are warmer and its winds are lighter. Its ice begins to break up and move. Some say the moving of ice sounds like a train. Some say the cracking ice sounds like singing whales. Either way, it is the sound of an Arctic summer on its way.

By June, the days grow longer and brighter. The temperature is above freezing. The yellow Arctic poppies bloom. Swarms of bugs are born. By June 22, the summer solstice arrives—the longest day of the year. On that day, above the Arctic Circle, the sun stays in the sky for a full twenty-four hours. That is why they call this region "the land of the midnight sun."

At first, the Arctic may look empty. "Nothing could survive so much cold and ice," you might say. But if that is what you think, you are wrong. Take the "king of the Arctic ice," the polar bear. The polar bear is one of the largest meat-eating mammals in the world. It can stand eight feet high and weigh over one thousand pounds. Like other Arctic mammals, the polar bear's fur is thick. But its hairs are almost see-through. This lets warm sunlight reach down to its black skin to keep it warm.

You will find walruses here too. You can spot
them on large floating pieces of ice. Walruses live in
shallow waters. When they are hungry, they dive
down to feed off the ocean floor. They feel for their
dinner of clams with their long whiskers.

Some people have gotten used to the cold. Once many called these Arctic people "Eskimos." That name means "eaters of raw fish." Today, these Arctic people like to be called "Inuit." It means "the people." The Inuit know how to live in a land of raw cold all year long.

The Inuit know the secret of warm clothes. They take two layers of heavy fur. One layer of fur faces the skin. Another layer faces out. Together, these layers keep out wind and water.

The Inuit know how to build igloos, houses made of blocks of snow. They carefully carve each block of snow with a large knife or saw. Snow blocks fit together to make walls and a ceiling. This keeps the cold out.

The Arctic, like every other region on Earth, has pollution. Oil wells have been drilled on the land. There have been oil spills. Birds and seals have died because of them.

Scientists have found that Arctic waters are polluted. Chemicals have traveled by water or air from hundreds of miles away. In warmer climates, these chemicals might disappear quickly. But in the cold Arctic air, the chemicals can remain for years.

Your Arctic adventure has come to an end. You have met the land, the animals, and the people. The Arctic is one of Earth's last great wild places. We must protect the air, water, and wildlife of the Arctic—the crown of the world.